Overcoming Ungodly Fear

Overcoming Ungodly Fear

by
Rebekah Prewitt

LakeCityCounsel.com

Other Resources

<u>by Rebekah Prewitt</u>
I'm Thinking of Leaving My Husband
Women Pastors
The Proper Role of the Wife: An Academic Study
Dealing With Suicide
How to Talk to Your Child About Divorce

<u>by Billy Prewitt</u>
The Pentecostal Commentary: Matthew
The Pentecostal Commentary: Galatians
Evidence for Speaking in Tongues
The Baptism in the Holy Spirit
What if Calvin Was Wrong?
Why Children Cry
The Inspiration of Scripture
Abraham

Trinity Bible School

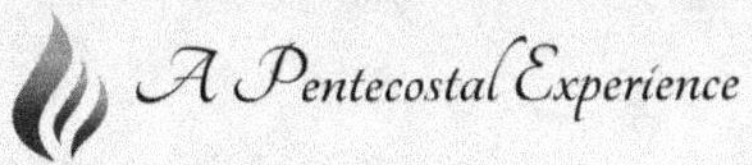

A Pentecostal Experience

QUALITY CHRISTIAN EDUCATION
PROVIDED REMOTELY
AT AN EXCEPTIONAL PRICE!

Trinity Bible School provides quality remote Christian training to believers who desire to be equipped and effective in working for the Lord. Whether you are a beginner or a degreed professional, we have courses designed for you. You can...

- Earn a Diploma of Biblical Studies in only one year

or

- Pursue an Associate, Bachelor, or Master level degree

To learn more, visit

TrinityBibleSchool.com

Contents

Introduction

"You must not shoot the devils, make them an offering of flour."[1] These were the words of an African king spoken to Henry Johnston. Johnston was a missionary during the late 1800s who traveled to Sierra Leone, West Africa to evangelize the lost. His experience with the people there taught him that the Africans were full of fear of the devils. To appease them, they brought gifts, not that they believed the devils were good, but out of fear of what they might do to them if they did not.

Fear is certainly no respecter of persons. It cares nothing for race or a person's status in life. Whole nations are bound by it, and the smallest child can face its debilitating effects. It is, however, important to note that not all fear is necessarily bad fear. There are certain fears that are healthy fears. For instance, it is good to have fear of touching a hot stove, playing with fire, or of petting dangerous animals. Even the Lord, speaking of leviathan, that great dragon or dinosaur, suggested to Job, "Wilt thou play with him as with a bird? or wilt thou bind him for thy maidens?" (Job 41:5). There is also the fear of jumping off of a high cliff. These are all examples of natural fears God built into man's system to protect him from harm. Speaking of leviathan again, the Lord said to Job, "Upon earth there is not his like, who is made without fear" (Job 41:33).

In addition to man's natural and healthy fears, there is also the fear that man needs to have of God or godly fear. This kind of fear needs to be in tact in every Christian's life. It is the fear of offending God in wrong doing, fear of God's majesty and glory, fear of His judgments and hell, and the fear of God's presence. John Bevere wrote,

> Fearing Him means to give Him the place of glory, honor, reverence, thanksgiving, praise and preeminence He deserves. (Notice it is what He deserves, not what we think He deserves). He holds this position in our lives when we esteem Him and His desires over and above our own. We will hate what He hates and love what He loves, trembling in His presence and at His word.[2]

Godly fear is also part of God's design to keep man from harm. Both natural and godly fear are good and necessary fears, but these are not the kinds of fear this book will address. This book will address the fear that suddenly grips a person and holds them captive. It addresses fear that causes a person's heartbeat to speed up when they have to deal with an uncomfortable situation. It addresses fear that paralyzes a person and inhibits them from operating normally as well as fear that pushes a person to flee in haste. It addresses the fear that hurts a person instead of preventing them from hurt. In other words, this book addresses unhealthy and ungodly fear.

In both natural fears and the proper fear of God, there is peace, but ungodly fear robs its subjects of peace. What exactly is this kind of fear, and from where does it come? Is it possible to really have victory over fear, or do we have to suffer with its repeated visits in our lives? In the chapters to follow, we will examine the subject of fear in light of the Scripture and analyze its effects and consequences. The reader will then be introduced to several useful approaches in overcoming ungodly fear. There may be certain struggles in life that can be ignored or even tempered. Fear is not one of those struggles. Rather, fear must be overcome.

Chapter 1

The Beginnings of Fear

It is said that history repeats itself, with that being the case, then a look backwards will be helpful in understanding this subject of fear. The very first time we see fear entering into the world was back in the Garden of Eden. It was in the beginning of creation that man was introduced to fear. According to the account in Genesis chapter three, after Adam and Eve ate the forbidden fruit,

The eyes of them both were opened, and they knew that they were naked; and they sewed fig leaves together, and made themselves aprons. And they heard the voice of the LORD God walking in the garden in the cool of the day: and Adam and his wife hid themselves from the presence of the LORD God amongst the trees of the garden. And the LORD God called unto Adam, and said unto him, Where art thou? And he said, I heard thy voice in the garden, and I was afraid, because I was naked; and I hid myself. And he said, Who told thee that thou wast naked? Hast thou eaten of the tree, whereof I commanded thee that thou shouldest not eat? (Genesis 3:7-11).

The first time mankind recognized fear was when they were naked. As one can observe, it did not take long for fear to intrude on the world. It originated with the very first people God ever created—Adam and Eve. John Wesley noted, "Shame and fear seized the criminals, these came into the world along with sin, and still attend it."[1] Prior to man's disobedience, God gave the command to Adam and said,

Of every tree of the garden thou mayest freely eat: But of the tree of the knowledge of good and evil, thou shalt not eat of it: for in the day that thou eatest thereof thou shalt surely die (Genesis 2:16-17).

Since the issuance of that command and the breaking of it, mankind plunged headlong into the downward spiral that they were never able to recover from by themselves. As a result, fear has plagued man for six thousand years. When man took hold of "the tree of the knowledge of good and evil" and ate, for "she took of the fruit thereof, and did eat, and gave also unto her husband with her; and he did eat" (3:6), the knowledge of fear was revealed to them. Prior to that, they had no concept of what fear was or how it felt. We know this to be true because after God created the woman and gave her to Adam as his wife, the Bible says, "And they were both naked, the man and his wife, and were not ashamed" (Genesis 2:25). They suffered no guilt for being naked then. Matthew Henry wrote,

> An evidence of the purity and innocency of that state wherein our first parents were created, Gen_2:25. They were both naked. They needed no clothes for defense against cold nor heat, for neither could be injurious to them. They needed none for ornament. Solomon in all his glory was not arrayed like one of these. Nay, they needed none for decency; they were naked, and had no reason to be ashamed. They knew not what shame was, so the Chaldee reads it. Blushing is now the colour of virtue, but it was not then the colour of innocency. Those that had no sin in their conscience might well

have no shame in their faces, though they had no clothes to their backs.[2]

When Adam and Eve disobeyed, not only did they break God's law, but through breaking of the law they obtained knowledge of good and evil illegally. Kenneth Matthews, a Bible commentator, points out, "This autonomous action meant death because this wisdom was obtained unlawfully."[3] If for instance, someone steals a certain piece of clothing, can they really be able to enjoy that thing, or will it be a constant reminder of their crime? Proverbs teaches, "In the transgression of an evil man there is a snare: but the righteous doth sing and rejoice" (29:6). Similarly, obtaining the knowledge of good and evil unlawfully brought man into a snare. It was not his to take. It was to be given by God, but because man took it illegally, man has reaped all the evils that come with it. Through this one act of disobedience to God, Adam has passed down fear. It has crept into the heart of man, and since that time, man has been reacting to it.

Chapter 2

What Is fear?

After looking at the beginnings of fear, the question of the nature of fear needs to be answered. Looking back to the inquisition recorded in Genesis chapter three between God and man, it was clear that there were three voices present in the Garden. One of those voices was the voice of the serpent.

"And the LORD God said unto the woman, What is this that thou hast done? And the woman said, The serpent beguiled me, and I did eat" (3:13). It was to this incident that the Apostle Paul refers when he said to the Corinthians, "But I fear, lest by any means, as the serpent beguiled Eve through his subtilty, so your minds should be corrupted from the simplicity that is in Christ" (2 Corinthians 11:3). We further learn who this serpent really is in the book of Revelation. John, the apostle, wrote, "And the great dragon was cast out, that old serpent, called the Devil, and Satan, which deceiveth the whole world: he was cast out into the earth, and his angels were cast out with him" (12:9). Henry notes, "The tempter, and that was the devil, in the shape and likeness of a serpent."[1] The serpent in the Garden was empowered by the devil himself who encouraged man to disobey God. The question then still remains, what exactly is fear?

When Jesus sent out his disciples to heal the sick, they returned and said to Jesus, "Lord, even the devils are subject unto us through thy name" (Luke 10:17). Jesus then told them, "I beheld Satan as lightning fall from heaven . . . Notwithstanding in this rejoice not, that the spirits are subject unto you; but rather rejoice, because your names are written in heaven" (Luke 10:18, 20). Here one can see that Jesus equated these devils to spirits. The Apostle Paul then later taught, "For God hath not given us the spirit of fear; but of power, and of love, and of a sound mind" (2 Timothy 1:7).

Based on these passages, Satan and his angels are spirits. If that is the case, then what Paul said to Timothy is important to understand about the subject of fear. There are two things one can learn about fear from Paul. First, God did not give man the spirit of fear. Second, fear is a spirit. This spirit had to have been one of Satan's angels that fell with him. We know that fallen angels are demons and Pastor Annacondia explains "demons are evil beings who have no material bodies, and they go around looking for a place in which to dwell. They speak, they reason, they see, and they hear."[2] In the next chapter, we will look at the various ways in which this evil spirit of fear manifests itself.

Chapter 3

Manifestations and Consequences of the Spirit of Fear

Again, referring back to the Garden of Eden when man was first introduced to the spirit of fear, there are several things to observe in the way this spirit operates. Based on the Genesis account, it is said,

> And the LORD God called unto Adam, and said unto him, Where art thou? And he said, I heard thy voice in the garden, and I was afraid, because I was naked; and I hid myself (Genesis 3:9-10).

The two verses prior state,

> And the eyes of them both were opened, and they knew that they were naked; and

they sewed fig leaves together, and made themselves aprons. And they heard the voice of the LORD God walking in the garden in the cool of the day: and Adam and his wife hid themselves from the presence of the LORD God amongst the trees of the garden (Genesis 3:7-8).

It is quite easy to observe that the spirit of fear drove man to three things. First, it caused man to react immediately. Adam did not sit around and reason what to do. He recognized his plight and was moved into immediate action. Second, because of fear, he covered himself. Fear led him to invent his own way of covering himself, which simply was not good enough. Third, man hid himself from God. Fear of facing God tormented Adam. Henry observes, "Fear is known to be a disquieting torturing passion, especially such a fear as is the dread of an almighty avenging God."[1] These three observable actions will be evident in one way or the other in the manifestations that follow.

Lies

Another early example of fear was displayed in the life of the patriarch Abraham and his family. On two occasions, Abraham was afraid to say that

Sarah was his wife. Instead, he said she was his sister prompted by the spirit of fear (Genesis 12:10-13; 20:2). His wife, Sarah, also acted in fear. Sarah had overheard that she was going to have a child in her old age. At this news, she laughed, but when she was questioned by the Lord, listen to her response. "Then Sarah denied, saying, I laughed not; for she was afraid. And he said, Nay; but thou didst laugh" (Genesis 18:15). Abraham and Sarah's son, Isaac, also evidenced the spirit of fear. The Bible records,

> And Isaac dwelt in Gerar: And the men of the place asked him of his wife; and he said, She is my sister: for he feared to say, She is my wife; lest, said he, the men of the place should kill me for Rebekah; because she was fair to look upon (Genesis 26:6-7).

In addition, in all four gospel accounts, Peter's bout with the spirit of fear is recorded. Peter was questioned three times after Jesus' arrest about being one of Jesus' disciples. On each occasion, Peter lied denying his acquaintance with the Lord (Matthew 26:69-75, Mark 14:66-72, Luke 22:54-62, and John 18:15-27). In each of these cases, the spirit of fear was at work prompting men to speak lies.

Worry

After Abraham sent away Hagar and their son, Ishmael, from his house. Hagar was in distress when her sustenance ran out. The Bible tells us that

> she cast the child under one of the shrubs. And she went, and sat her down over against him a good way off, as it were a bowshot: for she said, Let me not see the death of the child. And she sat over against him, and lift up her voice, and wept And God heard the voice of the lad; and the angel of God called to Hagar out of heaven, and said unto her, What aileth thee, Hagar? fear not; for God hath heard the voice of the lad where he is (Genesis 21:15-17).

Fear prompted Hagar to worry over her circumstances. This was a similar worry that the widow in Zarephath experienced.

It was a time of sore famine in Israel, but the prophet Elijah asked the widow in Zarephath for water and bread to eat. The widow said to him,

> As the LORD thy God liveth, I have not a cake, but an handful of meal in a barrel, and a little oil in a cruse: and, behold, I am gathering two sticks, that I

may go in and dress it for me and my son, that we may eat it, and die (1 Kings 17:12).

Elijah said to her, "Fear not; go and do as thou hast said: but make me thereof a little cake first, and bring it unto me, and after make for thee and for thy son" (1 Kings 17:13). This woman was prompted by fear to see only her immediate need, and this caused her to worry.

Speaking of her own personal struggles with worrying, radio teacher, Elisabeth Elliot, mentioned on her program a quotation by George MacDonald that has greatly helped her. MacDonald astutely pointed out,

> The care that is filling your mind at this moment, or but waiting till you lay the book aside to leap upon you—that need which is no need, is a demon sucking at the spring of your life. 'No; mine is a reasonable care—an unavoidable care, indeed.' Is it something you have to do this very moment? 'No.' Then you are allowing it to usurp the place of something that is required of you this moment. 'There is nothing required of me at this moment.' Nay but there is— the greatest thing that can be required of man. 'Pray, what is it?' Trust in the

living God... 'I do trust Him in spiritual matters.' Everything is an affair of the spirit.[2]

MacDonald has precisely diagnosed the root of worry. When a person starts worrying, it opens the door for the person to come under a spiritual attack of the enemy. This spiritual attack is termed today a "panic attack," but it is called "sudden fear" in the Bible.

Sudden Fear

The book of Job records, "Therefore snares are round about thee, and sudden fear troubleth thee" (Job 22:10). The spirit of fear tends to operate with suddenness or swiftness, and it seizes up its subjects. To paint a picture in the readers mind of how this spirit operates, Webster defines the term "seize" in this way,

> 1. To fall or rush upon suddenly and lay hold on; or to gripe or grasp suddenly. The tiger rushes from the thicket and seizes his prey. A dog seizes an animal by the throat. The hawk seizes a chicken with his claws. The officer seizes a thief. 2. To take possession by force, with or without right.

To give a modern example of how sudden fear can work in a person's life, let's look at a case between Robert and Susan, a husband and wife.

Robert normally calls Susan every morning at 7:25 a.m. when he gets to work. On a few occasions, Robert has forgotten to call Susan, but he told her, "If I don't call, don't assume something bad has happened." She agreed, and they continued in their routine. One particular morning, however, as Susan was having a lovely day going about her morning chores, she recognized that Robert failed to call on time. Susan started to worry. She sent a text to Robert, but she received no answer. She remembered that Robert had told her, "If I don't call, don't assume something bad has happened." Susan waited a few minutes. After about half an hour, Susan called Robert's cell phone, but she got no answer. She decided to wait again, but in the waiting, she reasoned, *I better put my make-up on in case someone comes to tell me bad news, or in case I need to go and find him*. By this time, Susan's mind was working overtime. Susan started imagining the loss and all the tragic things that could have happened to Robert. She then tried calling his employer, but her call went to voicemail. She tried calling Robert's cell phone again, no answer. Finally, around 8 a.m., Robert called Susan. As soon as Susan heard Robert's voice, Susan burst into that deep, can't breathe, crying. She felt immediate relief knowing that Robert was alive and safe. This experience, however, shook up Susan's entire body leaving her feeling quite jolted and depleted for the rest of the day.

Webster defines panic as,

A sudden fright; particularly, a sudden fright without real cause, or terror inspired by a trifling cause or misapprehension of danger; as the troops were seized with a panic; they fled in a panic.

Based on Webster's definition, Susan most definitely played into the hands of this spirit of fear. The same fear that the Africans, mentioned earlier, let control them when they gave gifts to their devils. For the space of about thirty minutes, Susan was totally consumed with losing Robert. She dismissed what Robert had told her and could think of nothing else. She was seized with fear. One half hour in her day robbed her of an entire day of joyfulness.

To help illustrate how a person's physical body is affected by fear, Adam Clarke examined king Belshazzar's experienced with the hand writing on the wall mentioned in Daniel 5. He wrote,

> *The king's* countenance was changed - Here is a very natural description of fear and terror.
>
> 1. The face grows pale;
>
> 2. The mind becomes greatly agitated;
>
> 3. Pains seize on the lower part of the back and kidneys;
>
> 4. A universal tremor takes place, so that the knees smite against each other;
>
> 5. And lastly, either a syncope takes place, or the cry of distress is uttered, Dan_5:7: "The king cried."[3]

The Bible gives several examples of how sudden fear can cause man to panic. When Pharaoh and his army were closing in on the children of Israel at the Red Sea, "The children of Israel lifted up their eyes, and, behold, the Egyptians marched after them; and they were sore afraid" (Exodus 14:10). This is what they said to Moses.

> Because there were no graves in Egypt, hast thou taken us away to die in the wilderness? wherefore hast thou dealt thus with us, to carry us forth out of Egypt? Is not this the word that we did tell thee in Egypt, saying, Let us alone, that we may serve the Egyptians? For it had been better for us to serve the Egyptians, than that we should die in the wilderness (Exodus 14:10-12).

The children of Israel were seized with fear, had no where to run, and lost all hope.

As the Philistines pursued King Saul, he was so terrified that "Saul took a sword, and fell upon it" (1 Samuel 31:4). For fear, Saul murdered himself when he saw no hope of escape. His armour-bearer also did likewise (1 Samuel 31:5). The Psalmist, David, later wrote this verse, "When the waves of death compassed me, the floods of ungodly men made me afraid" (2 Samuel 22:5). Zimri, King of Israel, also murdered himself when he realized that his city was besieged. "He went into the palace of the king's house, and burnt the king's house over him with fire, and died" (1 Kings 16:18).

When the king of Syria came to capture the prophet Elisha, the Scriptures record that they came with "horses, and chariots, and a great host: and they came by night, and compassed the city about" (2 Kings 6:14). Can you imagine waking up after a good night's rest only to be surprised by an army at your door.

> And when the servant of the man of God was risen early, and gone forth, behold, an host compassed the city both with horses and chariots. And his servant said unto him, Alas, my master! how shall we do? (2 Kings 6:15).

Elisha's servant experienced immediate or sudden fear.

In looking at how sudden fear operates, several things are observable:

1. It makes the person dismiss reason or causes them to waver.

2. It totally dominates the person's thoughts with the thing they fear. This leads the person to operate with total lock-down, tunnel focused vision.

3. It puts the person under a spiritual attack.

4. It works quickly in the person's life.

5. It frightens the body causing it to be tense so that it can't relax.

Paralyzes

The spirit of fear also seeks to paralyze man. When Joshua sent the two spies to spy out the land of Jericho, the harlot Rahab told them,

> I know that the LORD hath given you the land, and that your terror is fallen upon us, and that all the inhabitants of the land faint because of you. . . And as soon as we had heard these things, our hearts did melt, neither did there remain any more courage in any man, because of you (Joshua 2:9, 11).

The Scriptures also mention, "Now Jericho was straitly shut up because of the children of Israel: none went out, and none came in" (Joshua 6:1). Due to fear, the whole city of Jericho was immobile or paralyzed.

Flee

In contrast to paralyzing man, the spirit of fear can motivate man to run or take flight. When

Jacob's father-in-law questioned him about leaving him so hastily, Jacob responded, "Because I was afraid: for I said, Peradventure thou wouldest take by force thy daughters from me" (Genesis 31:31). After Moses killed an Egyptian for hurting a Hebrew, Moses feared and fled to the land of Midian (Exodus 2:14). When the Philistines came against the armies of Israel with their champion Goliath, the men of Israel "fled from him, and were sore afraid" (1 Samuel 17:24). At the time Jesus was arrested, for fear of being captured themselves, "All the disciples forsook him, and fled" (Matthew 26:56). Fear will cause man to run from an uncomfortable situation.

Torment

The Apostle John tells us, "Fear hath torment" (1 John 4:18). Webster defines torment as, "To put to extreme pain or anguish; to inflict excruciating pain and misery, either of body or mind." This torment was felt by Jacob after stealing his brother's blessing. On his journey home from Haran, Jacob was terribly afraid to face his brother, Esau. So much so that, he wrestled with God all night and prayed, "Deliver me, I pray thee, from the hand of my brother, from the hand of Esau: for I fear him, lest he will come and smite me, and the mother with the children" (Genesis 32:11). As a result of his fear, Jacob set his family and his servants in bands and sent present after present ahead of him in hopes of appeasing his brother's wrath. Jacob's fear tormented him because he had done his brother wrongly. Joseph Exell observed, "The consciousness of crime begets terror; for 'the wicked flee when no one pursueth.'"[4]

Cower

Fear will make a man behave cowardly. When the Lord told Gideon to go and smash his father's idol and cut down his images, the Scripture records,

> Then Gideon took ten men of his servants, and did as the LORD had said unto him: and so it was, because he feared his father's household, and the men of the city, that he could not do it by day, that he did it by night (Judges 6:27).

The Apostle Peter had a similar experience. The Apostle Paul confronted the Apostle Peter as Peter once again battled with this spirit of fear. Paul wrote:

But when Peter was come to Antioch, I withstood him to the face, because he was to be blamed. For before that certain came from James, he did eat with the Gentiles: but when they were come, he withdrew and separated himself, fearing them which were of the circumcision (Galatians 2:11-12).

Fear will cause men to cower and not be brave. Alexander MacLaren stated well when he said,

'God hath not given us the spirit of cowardice.' Now, of course, courage or timidity are very largely matters of temperament. But then, you know, the very purpose of the gospel is to mend temperaments, to restrain, and to stimulate, so as that natural defects may become excellences, and excellences may never run to seed and become defects. So whilst we have to admit that religion is not meant to obliterate natural distinctions in character, we must also remember that we insufficiently grasp the intention of the gospel which we say we believe unless we realise that it is meant to deal with the most deeply rooted defects in character, to make the crooked things straight, and the rough places plain.[5]

Intimidates

The man Nehemiah was a fearless man and perhaps that is why he was chosen by the Lord to help rebuild the wall in Jerusalem. Howbeit, Nehemiah was put in a position to be intimidated by Tobias and Sanballat on several occasions. This is how Nehemiah responded when the spirit of fear sought to intimidate him.

> For they all made us afraid, saying, Their hands shall be weakened from the work, that it be not done. Now therefore, O God, strengthen my hands. Afterward I came unto the house of Shemaiah the son of Delaiah the son of Mehetabeel, who was shut up; and he said, Let us meet together in the house of God, within the temple, and let us shut the doors of the temple: for they will come to slay thee; yea, in the night will they come to slay thee. And I said, Should such a man as I flee? and who is there, that, being as I am, would go into the temple to save his life? I will not go in. And, lo, I perceived that God had not sent him;

but that he pronounced this prophecy against me: for Tobiah and Sanballat had hired him (Nehemiah 6:9-12).

Nehemiah understood that he should not focus on himself and saving his own life. Bevere notes, "What is going to happen to me? This is how intimidation will change your focus. The reason: The root of intimidation is fear, and fear causes people to focus on themselves."[6]

If a person is afraid to deal with something, then they may delay that task. This is the spirit of fear trying to intimidate that person from accomplishing that thing. The story of Rabshakeh also comes to mind. When Rabshakeh made his bold speech to the house of Judah and spoke against the Living God, his aim was to make them afraid, cease their work, and surrender to the king of Assyria (2 Kings 18:17-37).

Move

Fear will look to move one's heart. It seeks to dislodge a person from their place of stability. In other words, it makes one unstable or shifty. It causes a person to waver in their decision making. When King Ahaz learned that the Northern

Kingdom of Israel had joined with the Syrians and that they were coming to fight against the house of Judah, the Bible records, "And it was told the house of David, saying, Syria is confederate with Ephraim. And his heart was moved, and the heart of his people, as the trees of the wood are moved with the wind" (Isaiah 7:2). Fear can also move a person's heart when they hear bad news of a certain health condition, some kind of deformity in their unborn child, or anything that the enemy can use to dislodge them. Margaret Hicks wrote, "Satan moves in at this critical time and uses tools of fear and anxiety with cruel results."[7]

Confederate

Fear will make a person seek alliances with others for protection. This was seen in the lives of Ahaz and Barak. When Barak heard that he was to go and fight with Sisera, Barak said to Deborah, the judge of Israel, "If thou wilt go with me, then I will go: but if thou wilt not go with me, then I will not go" (Judges 4:8). Robert Hawker, however, disagrees that Barak was showing fear. He wrote,

> I do not think that Barak, by this answer,
> manifested fear; but rather, it arose from
> the confidence he had, that by her

accompanying him, the people would be the more convinced that the thing was of the Lord.[8]

John Darby argued, "Barak has faith enough to obey if he has some one near who can lean immediately on God, but not enough to do so himself."[9]

In relation to Ahaz in his time of desperation, fear prompted him to join with Assyria for help.

> So Ahaz sent messengers to Tiglathpileser king of Assyria, saying, I am thy servant and thy son: come up, and save me out of the hand of the king of Syria, and out of the hand of the king of Israel, which rise up against me (2 Kings 16:7).

The Ultimate Consequence

Everything we have seen can be viewed as a consequence of fear, but in each of those manifestations, the repercussions were immediate. The ultimate consequence of yielding to the spirit of fear is written in the book of Revelation. Jesus says,

> But the fearful, and unbelieving, and the abominable, and murderers, and whoremongers, and sorcerers, and idolaters, and all liars, shall have their part in the lake which burneth with fire and brimstone: which is the second death (Revelation 21:8).

In this list of abominable sins fear is listed first and will prevent a person's entrance into heaven. This would be the ultimate consequence. A fearful person is not going to heaven. This should alert every person struggling with fear to overcome this spirit in their lives. Referencing this same verse, Hicks shared,

> When I first saw that, I was amazed, I had always felt pity for people who were fearful and apprehensive. But fear in the heart of a believer must be a repulsive sight to God. . . For a believer to fall back in fear when his faith is tested must cause our heavenly Father a deep hurt.[10]

In the next chapter, we will look at several ways to overcoming this spirit.

Chapter 4

Overcoming the Spirit of Fear

Fortunately, God, through His Son, Jesus Christ, has made it possible for man to overcome the spirit of fear. As discussed in chapter two, fear is a spirit, and it is not a holy spirit. Unless this spirit is dealt with properly, we will forever abide in fear and feel shame for giving the devil place in our lives.

An interesting observation worth noting is that spirits are not easy to pin down. They are shifty. One moment they will attack a person in one way, and the next moment in a different way. In this chapter, we will look at several approaches to overcoming the unholy spirit of fear.

Recognition

The first step in dealing with the spirit of fear is recognition. Sometimes you are not immediately conscious that you are operating in fear. By the time you realize what is happening, you have already made several blunders. If, however, you identify your enemy early, then you will know how to deal with him quickly. This is critical. You must know who it is you are facing. People who fall into this spirit's trap over and over again will do well to pray a simple prayer of asking the Lord to help them recognize when they are operating in fear. This will be a triumphant beginning in tackling this giant.

Repentance

After you recognize that you are operating or have operated in fear, the next step is to repent. Repentance closes the door to that evil spirit's work in your life. When a person operates in fear he or she is not being led by the Holy Spirit any longer but by an evil spirit. The evil spirit of fear is the one calling the shots at that moment. When we operate in fear, we are allowing an unholy spirit to lead us, and Satan gains a foothold in our lives. "Know ye not, that to whom ye yield yourselves servants to obey, his servants ye are to whom ye obey" (Romans 6:16). We do not have to be a servant of fear any longer. We can start to overcome this spirit by repenting for operating in it.

The other reason for repentance is that people who are operating in the spirit of fear are also operating without faith. Paul says, "For whatsoever is not of faith is sin" (Romans 14:23). Whatever situation you may be facing, you lack the confidence that God can help you through it. "Fear and unbelief are tied together. They are considered by God to be a great evil. Why? Because they make of none effect all the great promises of God."[1] Repentance, therefore, is necessary.

Yet, another reason for repentance is that possibly people who are fearful have other specific sins that they have not properly handled. Noah Webster calls this slavish fear which is the effect or consequence of guilt. He says, it is the painful apprehension of merited punishment. Remember, this ungodly spirit of fear made its entrance into man's life when man disobeyed God, and his disobedience brought a snare upon him. So, if you are feeling guilty for some sin you committed, whether it be against your Creator or your neighbor, this guilt will lead to fear. This fear, however, can be vanquished when you take the right action. Psalm

86:5 states, "For thou, Lord, *art* good, and ready to forgive; and plenteous in mercy unto all them that call upon thee." Another Psalm states, "The LORD *is* merciful and gracious, slow to anger, and plenteous in mercy" (Psalms 103:8). God is indeed merciful and is ready to forgive. I can testify of this in my own life.

Sometime ago, I had the following thought during my prayer time, *If I had messed up like I had today and had no way to remedy my relationship with God, what would I have done? I would be in agony all the time.* Our God is a gentle God, unlike us. He does not chasten with a heavy hand when we have erred. Rather, I have noticed that He will drop a spiritual thought into my mind (Spirit of prophecy) that causes me to examine myself. He says, "As many as I love, I rebuke and chasten: be zealous therefore, and repent" (Revelation 3:19).

Cast out

Several years ago, a Christian woman went to see a Christian counselor because she was struggling with fear. She said to the counselor, "I am struggling with fear, and I am hearing voices in other rooms. I am on medication for fear that makes me feel sedated. What should I do with this?" The counselor asked her if she had recently had her hearing checked by a doctor. She said, "Yes, and my hearing is fine." The counselor then directed her to 2 Timothy 1:7. She read, "For God hath not given us the spirit of fear; but of power, and of love, and of a sound mind."

The counselor asked, "What is fear?"

She said, "A spirit."

The counselor then asked, "How do you fix a spirit with drugs?"

People struggling with this kind of fear are not wrestling with a physical difficulty. The problem is not with their head or their heart. God gave us a "sound mind" and "love." This kind of fear is of a spiritual nature. It does not have a corporeal presence. In other words, it does not have a body. It is a spirit, and this spirit looks for a body to inhabit. Taking medication for fear only seeks to numb the person's senses, but that spirit is still alive and well. He is ready to be released through the motions of the flesh after the drugs taper off.

My husband works with children, and quite often, they are on medicine. He has noticed that when they are on their medication, they are docile, but if their parents forget to give them their medication, they become wild. Were the children healed after taking the medication? No. They were simply sedated. Medicine could not fix the children's problems. Christ, however, did not come to cover over our problems giving us a pseudo relief, but He came to set us free from the power of the devil. This ungodly spirit must be cast out.

When Sarah saw Hagar's son mocking Isaac, Sarah told Abraham, "Cast out this bondwoman and her son: for the son of this bondwoman shall not be heir with my son, even with Isaac" (Genesis 21:10). This was the first time we see in Scripture this phrase "cast out." As the child of the flesh had to be cast out, so this ungodly spirit cannot occupy any space in our lives. It must be cast out. Commanding the spirit of fear to leave in name of Jesus is important to do.

Readjust

Next, one must readjust their actions and behaviors to match the normal course of events. In dealing with fear, the action you take is more important than the way you feel. The feelings of fear may be present, but if you take the right action, you will no longer be operating by the spirit of fear.

Stand Still

We have learned that fear likes to make people cower and flee. If, for instance, you recognize that you normally flee from an uncomfortable situation, then this is the time to stand still.

When the Egyptians were in hot pursuit of the children of Israel, the Israelites were terrified, but Moses' advice to them was, "Fear ye not, stand still, and see the salvation of the LORD, which he will shew to you to day" (Exodus 14:13). Standing still may not require a word to be said, yet your position should be one of stillness and not of flight.

One day, for the first time, I saw myself like the Apostle Peter in the following light. Peter drew back from the Lord when He was arrested. He sat by the door so as to distance himself from Christ, and I did similarly. While at the store with my husband, he became engaged in confronting a man over the issue of suicide. Fearing the confrontation, I gradually stepped further and further back from my husband. The fear of the confrontation weighed so intensely on me that I fled. Instead, I should have stood still. The prophet Isaiah said, "Their strength *is* to sit still" (Isaiah 30:7). What a lesson to learn, yet it is a lesson I have had to be reminded of frequently.

When we are in intense fear, there is also the temptation to talk excessively. If you find that you are afraid of a certain person, thing, or situation, refuse to speak. Unless you can speak in faith, HOLD YOUR TONGUE, and be still.

The spirit of fear operates in intensity. It likes to put pressure on its subjects to react immediately —even in something like running to the doctor. Early one morning, I was awaken by a throbbing pain in my big right toe. The toe was swollen and red. The problem surfaced overnight. I immediately went into the pantry and found some oil and applied it to the swollen area. My next thought, as you can imagine, was to go to the doctor, but in learning to be still, I was reminded that Jesus told Martha, "Said I not unto thee, that, if thou wouldest believe, thou shouldest see the glory of God?" (John 11:40).

Over and again, I hear of people who are pressured into having a surgery. There is always a sense of urgency in the matter. Those that place this pressure act as if the person is going to die immediately if he or she is not rushed into the operating room. I have learned, however, that this is how the enemy operates. He comes in like a flood, like a swarm with force and intense urging. This is the spirit of fear at work and not the Lord of peace operating in your life. The Bible says, "When the enemy shall come in like a flood, the Spirit of the

LORD shall lift up a standard against him" (Isaiah 59:19). "Be still, and know that I *am* God: I will be exalted among the heathen, I will be exalted in the earth" (Psalm 46:10).

Being still, which is necessary if you are tempted to flee or make a move, does not mean that you are to be paralyzed. Being still is a deliberate confrontational stance you take to ward off your enemy even though you may not be doing anything. There is an interesting fact known about the moose. It is said of the moose that wolves like to keep them running so as to make them weary. However, an older moose will often just stand and wait for the wolves to approach. When the wolves realize that this moose is not going to flee, they back off. Paul writes, "Wherefore take unto you the whole armour of God, that ye may be able to withstand in the evil day, and having done all, to stand" (Ephesians 6:13). May we take up our rightful position, and stand!

Stand Still by Keeping With the Plan

When fear comes in and tries to move a person's heart, or tries to halt a work for the Lord as was the case with Nehemiah, the Psalmist encourages, "He shall not be afraid of evil tidings: his heart is fixed, trusting in the LORD" (Psalm 112:7). "Which holdeth our soul in life, and suffereth not our feet to be moved" (Psalm 66:9). Whatever business we have to do, we should not fear to do it no matter what threats may be proposed. We need to keep with the plan.

Recently, my husband and I took a brief vacation, but it was to be even more brief than I had planned. The evening before our departure, as I sat overlooking the water and reading a book, I happened to look over to the right of me only to see a poisonous snake a few feet from my chair. Stunned by his presence, I told my husband, who was fishing close by, "I think there is snake over there." I then rose up from the chair and backed away. I did not scream or run away like I would have normally done. My husband was surprised at my calmness in dealing with that situation. What he did not realize immediately, however, is that afterwards my heart was moved with fear. Even though I had taken the right actions initially, fear of that serpent caused me to cut short my vacation a day early. This was the wrong thing to do. I should not have allowed fear to alter my plans. I reasoned with it saying, *Well, we only have one more night here. What would it matter if I left one night early. I am planning to leave in the morning anyway.* This was another wrong thing to do. You cannot and should not reason with fear. If you have a predetermined plan, stick with the plan. This is another way to overcome this spirit.

Taking Action

Sometimes, instead of confronting fear by standing still, you have to confront fear by taking action. The situation necessitates it. Perhaps, you are afraid to deal with a certain matter and would love to pass it off to someone else to handle. Fear to deal with that particular situation is an indication that you have to deal with it yourself. How often doesn't a wife ask her husband to deal with something that she is afraid to confront—maybe it's a neighbor or someone at church. This fear cannot be passed off. It must be overcome.

You may remember Jether, the firstborn son of Gideon. After his father had captured the two kings of Midian, Zebah and Zalmunna, Gideon instructed Jether, "Up, *and* slay them. But the youth drew not his sword: for he feared, because he *was* yet a youth" (Judges 8:20). Placed in a position to learn the use of arms for his God and his country, he might have shared in the honor of the victory,[1] but Jether was robbed of these glorious opportunities because he stood still instead of taking action.

Remember the Word

When a person is afraid they are prone to doubt what they know to be true. Susan, mentioned earlier, was told by her husband not to assume something bad had happened to him, yet she overrode his voice. You cannot allow yourself to override what you have been told, or else sudden fear will have a field day with you.

Fear will try hard to make you waver or stagger, but you must remember the word that was given to you before hand. These very words will be what you need to hold on to when you are bombarded by this evil spirit. Whether it be a word spoken in the natural (like Susan's husband's words) or a spiritual word taken directly from the Bible, if it is given to you, do not shift from it. Remember the patriarch Abraham (Romans 4:18-22). He was given a word (a promise), and though everything around him looked dead,

> He staggered not at the promise of God through unbelief; but was strong in faith, giving glory to God; And being fully persuaded that, what he had promised, he was able also to perform.

God has given us His Word and when we use it rightly, it is "mighty through God to the pulling down of strong holds" (2 Corinthians 10:4). If, for example, your immediate reaction is to tell a lie when you are afraid, remember the Word which tells you "Stand therefore, having your loins girt about with truth" (Ephesians 6:14). Speak the truth regardless of what the consequences may be. In so doing, you will be armed to deal with this evil spirit versus telling a lie which exposes a hole in your armor against his attacks.

Below is a suggested list of sixteen Scripture verses to consider when dealing with the spirit of fear:

1. "I sought the LORD, and he heard me, and delivered me from all my fears" (Psalms 34:4).

2. "So that we may boldly say, The Lord is my helper, and I will not fear what man shall do unto me" (Hebrews 13:6).

3. "The LORD is my light and my salvation; whom shall I fear? the LORD is the strength of my life; of whom shall I be afraid?" (Psalm 27:1).

4. "In God have I put my trust: I will not be afraid what man can do unto me" (Psalms 56:11).

5. "And he answered, Fear not: for they that be with us are more than they that be with them" (2 Kings 6:16).

6. "But none of these things move me, neither count I my life dear unto myself, so that I might finish my course with joy, and the ministry, which I have received of the Lord Jesus, to testify the gospel of the grace of God" (Acts 20:24).

7. "Therefore will not we fear, though the earth be removed, and though the mountains be carried into the midst of the sea" (Psalms 46:2).

8. "Though an host should encamp against me, my heart shall not fear: though war should rise against me, in this will I be confident" (Psalms 27:3).

9. "Be not afraid of sudden fear, neither of the desolation of the wicked, when it cometh" (Proverbs 3:25).

10. "Fear thou not; for I am with thee: be not dismayed; for I am thy God: I will strengthen thee; yea, I will help thee; yea, I will uphold thee with the right hand of my righteousness" (Isaiah 41:10).

11. "He shall not be afraid of evil tidings: his heart is fixed, trusting in the LORD" (Psalms 112:7).

12. "For I the LORD thy God will hold thy right hand, saying unto thee, Fear not; I will help thee" (Isaiah 41:13).

13. "Even as Sara obeyed Abraham, calling him lord: whose daughters ye are, as long as ye do well, and are not afraid with any amazement" (1 Peter 3:6).

14. "Be still, and know that I *am* God" (Psalm 46:10a).

15. "Casting all your care upon him; for he careth for you" (1 Peter 5:7).

16. "Be careful for nothing; but in every thing by prayer and supplication with thanksgiving let your requests be made known unto God" (Philippians 4:6).

Love

The Apostle John said, "There is no fear in love; but perfect love casteth out fear: because fear hath torment. He that feareth is not made perfect in love" (1 John 4:18). Fear is cast out by perfect love. If a person's love is defective, then he or she will fear. When someone is terribly worried over a loved one, perhaps a parent over a child, this is not the time to say, *Oh, look how that mother really loves that child*. This is not love. There is no fear in perfect love. Perfect love entirely entrusts itself to God. It is confident that God will take care of whatever concerns may arise. Love of this nature requires that the person be regenerated. An unsaved person can never operate in perfect love. The Bible says that "God is love" (1 John 4:8). "And he that dwelleth in love dwelleth in God, and God in him. Herein is our love made perfect," (1 John 4:16-17a).

Love is also a fruit of the Spirit of God, and it is mentioned first in the list of Galatians 5:22. George O. Wood writes,

> The great thing about the fruit of the Spirit is that it operates in difficulties. It's really most clearly seen then. In writing to the Galatians, Paul knew they had seen the fruit of the Spirit in his life

when he had been under extreme pressure and adversity. In all kinds of situations, the Spirit of God is seeking to bear fruit in you.[2]

What an excellent statement by Woods. As Christians, if we are fearful, whether it be over a child, a person, or a situation, we must realize that God is working this trying circumstance to develop the fruit of love in our lives. Therefore, we should not resist it.

One day after reading the words of Peter, I was greatly encouraged. He said,

> Casting all your care upon him; for he careth for you. Be sober, be vigilant; because your adversary the devil, as a roaring lion, walketh about, seeking whom he may devour: Whom resist stedfast in the faith, knowing that the same afflictions are accomplished in your brethren that are in the world. But the God of all grace, who hath called us unto his eternal glory by Christ Jesus, after that ye have suffered a while, make you perfect, stablish, strengthen, settle you (1 Peter 5:7-10).

I was reminded that day that we go through these things so that we can be made "perfect, stablish, strengthen, and settle." I was also reminded that day that "The fining pot *is* for silver, and the furnace for gold: but the LORD trieth the hearts" (Proverbs 17:3). We may secretly be afraid of some thing or person, but we can't hide anything from the Lord; therefore, we should not try. Instead of resisting fear, we should study to learn how God would want us to overcome fear and do it, so we can be useful to Him.

Conclusion

Thank you for taking the time to read this book, I trust that it has been very helpful to you. To conclude, I would like to leave you with the sobering examples of two men who come to mind. Both were prophets of the Lord. Both were placed in a position to operate in fear. One overcame in spite of potentially losing his life, the other did not overcome and did lose his life. The two men are the prophets Jeremiah and Urijah. Both were sent to prophesy to the house of Judah. Jeremiah 26:11-14 records,

> Then spake the priests and the prophets unto the princes and to all the people, saying, This man is worthy to die; for he hath prophesied against this city, as ye have heard with your ears. Then spake Jeremiah unto all the princes and to all the people, saying, The LORD sent me to prophesy against this house and against this city all the words that ye have heard. Therefore now amend your ways and your doings, and obey the voice

of the LORD your God; and the LORD will repent him of the evil that he hath pronounced against you. As for me, behold, I am in your hand: do with me as seemeth good and meet unto you.

Of the other prophet, Urijah, the book of Jeremiah notes,

And there was also a man that prophesied in the name of the LORD, Urijah the son of Shemaiah of Kirjathjearim, who prophesied against this city and against this land according to all the words of Jeremiah: And when Jehoiakim the king, with all his mighty men, and all the princes, heard his words, the king sought to put him to death: but when Urijah heard it, he was afraid, and fled, and went into Egypt; And Jehoiakim the king sent men into Egypt, namely, Elnathan the son of Achbor, and certain men with him into Egypt. And they fetched forth Urijah out of Egypt, and brought him unto Jehoiakim the king; who slew him with the sword, and cast his dead body into the graves of the common people. Nevertheless the hand of Ahikam the son of Shaphan was with Jeremiah, that they should not give him into the hand of the people to put him to death (Jeremiah 26:20-24).

Commenting on this account, Henry writes,

As good examples, and the good consequences of them, should encourage us in that which is good, so the examples of bad men, and the bad consequences of them, should deter us from that which is evil. . . . When he heard that the king had become his enemy, and sought his life, he was afraid, and fled, and went in to Egypt. This was certainly his fault, and an effect of the weakness of his faith, and it sped accordingly. He distrusted God, and his power to protect him and bear him out; he was too much under the power of that fear of man which brings a snare. God wonderfully preserved Jeremiah, though he did not flee, as Urijah did, but stood his ground.[1]

We do not always take into consideration the seriousness of fear working in our lives, but the spirit of fear is no respecter of persons. It attacks young and old, male and female, rich and poor, and most certainly prophets of the Lord. It is an ugly giant that needs to be slayed. You can't run from it, reason with it, temper it, or appease it. The only way to deal with ungodly fear is to overcome it. When I think of overcoming something, I think of leaping across it. I am reminded of these words by the Psalmist's, "For by thee I have run through a troop; and by my God have I leaped over a wall" (Psalms 18:29). Through "The Prince of Peace" we shall do valiantly, subdue, and get the victory over the spirit of fear! I trust that after reading this brief book, you will be more equipped to do just that.

Notes

Introduction

1. Alberta R. Metz, *Henry W. Johnston* (Marion, IN: The Wesleyan Publishing House, 1978), 41.

2. John Bevere, *Breaking Intimidation* (Orlando, FL: Creation House, 1995), 142.

Chapter 1

1. John Wesley, *John Wesley's Notes on the Bible* (public domain, 1755-1766), Genesis 3:6-8.

2. Matthew Henry, *Matthew Henry's Commentary on the Bible* (public domain, 1708-1714), Genesis 2:21-25.

3. Kenneth A. Matthews, *The New American Commentary: An Exegetical and Theological Exposition of Holy Scripture, Genesis 1-11:26, Vol. 1A* (Broadman & Holman Publishers, 1996), 206.

Chapter 2

1. Matthew Henry, *Matthew Henry's Commentary on the Bible* (public domain, 1708-1714), Genesis 3:1-5.

2. Carlos Annacondia, *Listen to Me, Satan!* (Orlando, FL: Creation House, 1998), 45.

Chapter 3

1. Matthew Henry, *Matthew Henry's Commentary on the Bible* (public domain, 1708-1714), 1 John 4:17-21.

2. Gateway to Joy, "Restlessness," May 7, 2021.

3. Adam Clarke, *Adam Clark's Commentary on the Bible* (public domain, 1810-1826), Daniel 5:6.

4. Joseph S. Exell, *The Biblical Illustrator* (public domain, 1900), Genesis 3:7.

5. Alexander MacLaren, *Expositions of Holy Scripture* (public domain, 1904-1910), 2 Timothy 1:7.

6. John Bevere, *Breaking Intimidation* (Orlando, FL: Creation House, 1995), 17.

7. Margaret Hicks, *A Christian Woman's Answer to Aging* (Tulsa, OK: Harrison House, 1986), 14.

8. Robert Hawker, *Poor Man's Commentary* (public domain, 1805), Judges 4:8-9.

9. John Darby, *John Darby's Synopsis of the Bible* (public domain, 1857-1862), Judges 4:1-24.

10. Hicks, 13-14.

Chapter 4

1. John Wesley, *John Wesley's Notes on the Bible* (public domain, 1755-1766), Judges 8:20.

Notes

2. Donald Gee, *The Fruit of the Spirit*, (Springfield, MO: Gospel Publishing House, 2010), forward.

Conclusion

1. Matthew Henry, *Matthew Henry's Commentary on the Bible* (public domain, 1708-1714), Jeremiah 26:16-24.

About the Author

Rebekah Prewitt is the wife of Billy Prewitt. She is also a Bible-based Christian counselor and operates in North Florida, USA. Rebekah holds a Doctorate in Christian Counseling and is the author of several counseling resources. The Prewitts make their home in North Florida. To contact Rebekah Prewitt directly, visit LakeCityCounsel.com.